20个必学象形图字 - 2
习字及著色本

20 Must-learn Pictographic Simplified Chinese Workbook

2

Coloring, Handwriting, Pinyin

白雲

20 Must-Learn Pictographic Simplified Chinese Workbook 2
Coloring, Handwriting, Pinyin

Illustrated by Chris Huang
Edited by Iris Chiou
Proof Read by Maxine Yang
Published by Cloud Chinese
All copyrights © by Chuming Huang
Inside 44 pages Black & White
Paperback Color with Matte finished
Printed in US
ISBN 13 : 978-1-954729-93-3
Reference ID: 001
Language: : Chinese
Publication Date: 2021, March, 5th

Cloud Chinese, Wilmette, IL, USA
www.mycloudchinese.com
myeasyshows@gmail.com

TABLE OF CONTENTS

MOUTH

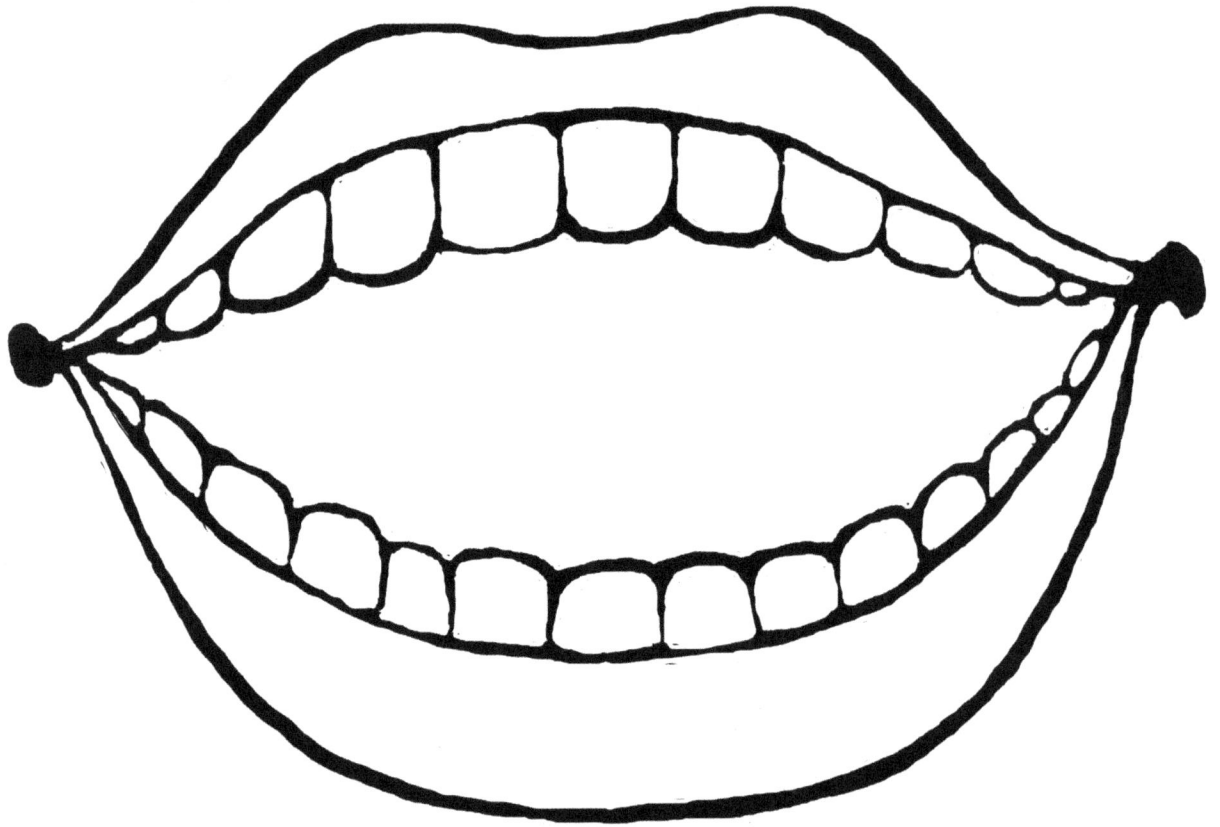

 kǒu

kǒu

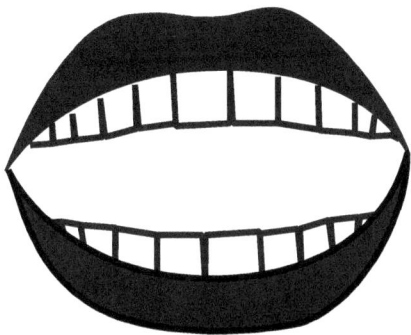

kāi kǒu

开 口

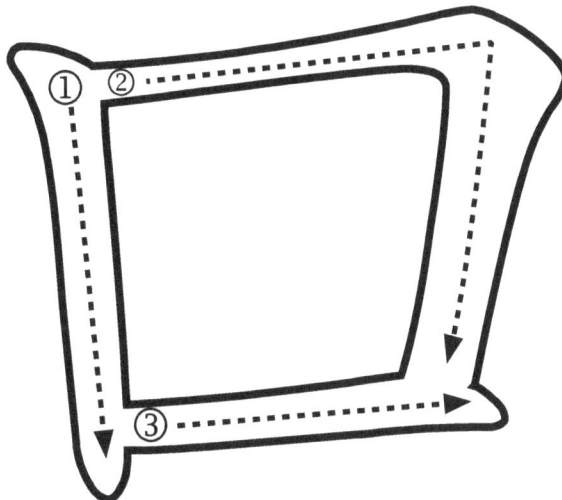

kǒu	kǒu	kǒu		
丨	冂	口		

LEFT

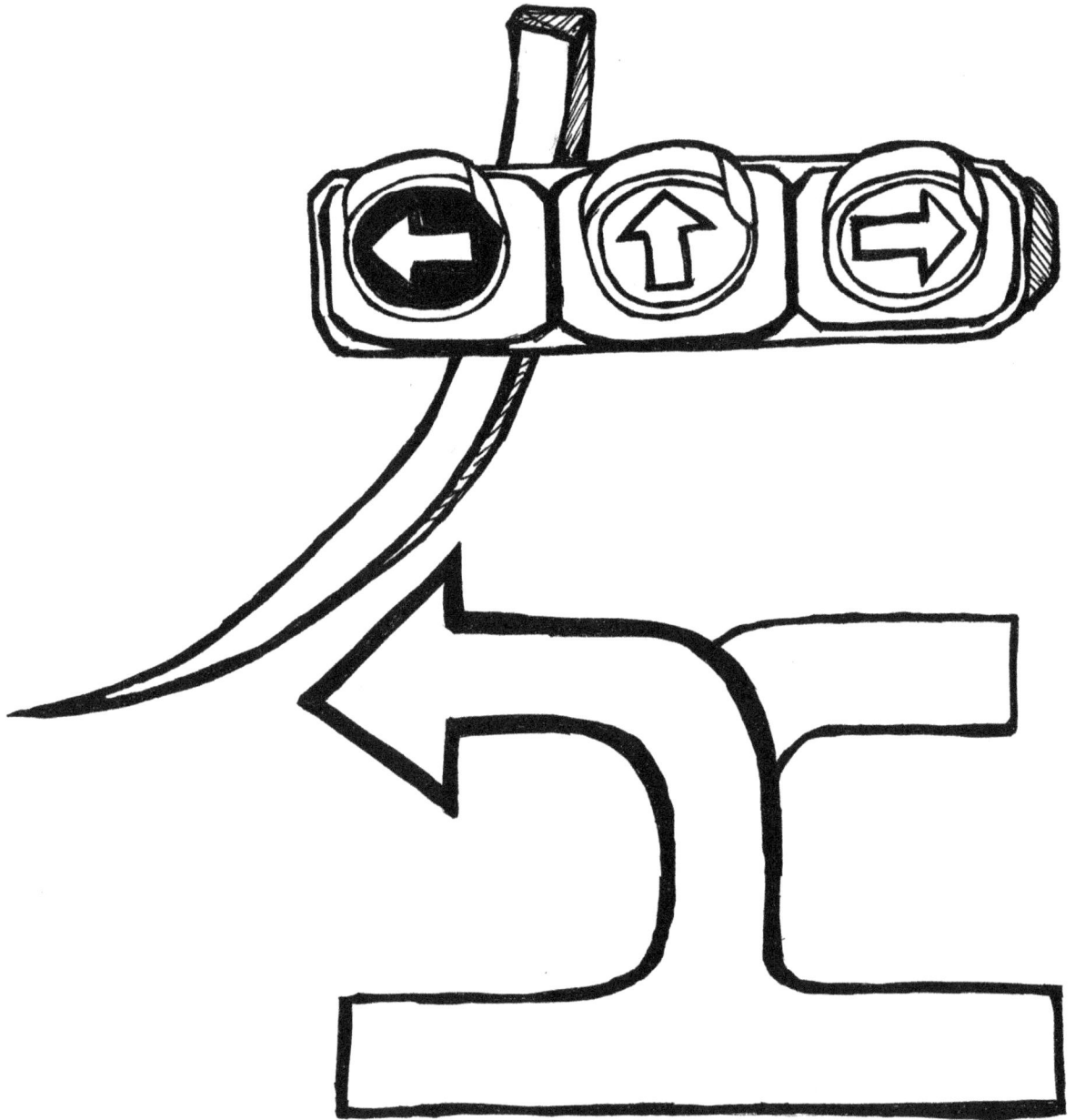

左

zuǒ

zuǒ zhuǎn

左转

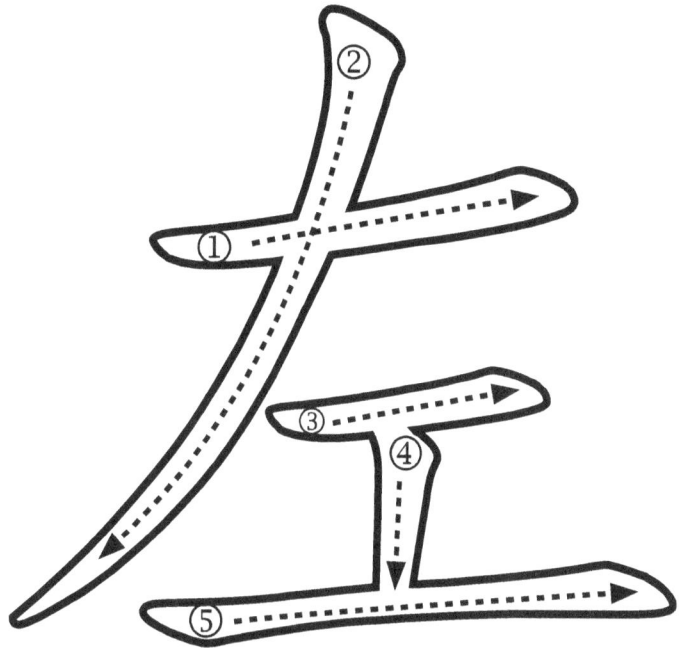

zuǒ	zuǒ	zuǒ	zuǒ	zuǒ
一	ナ	左	左	左

RIGHT

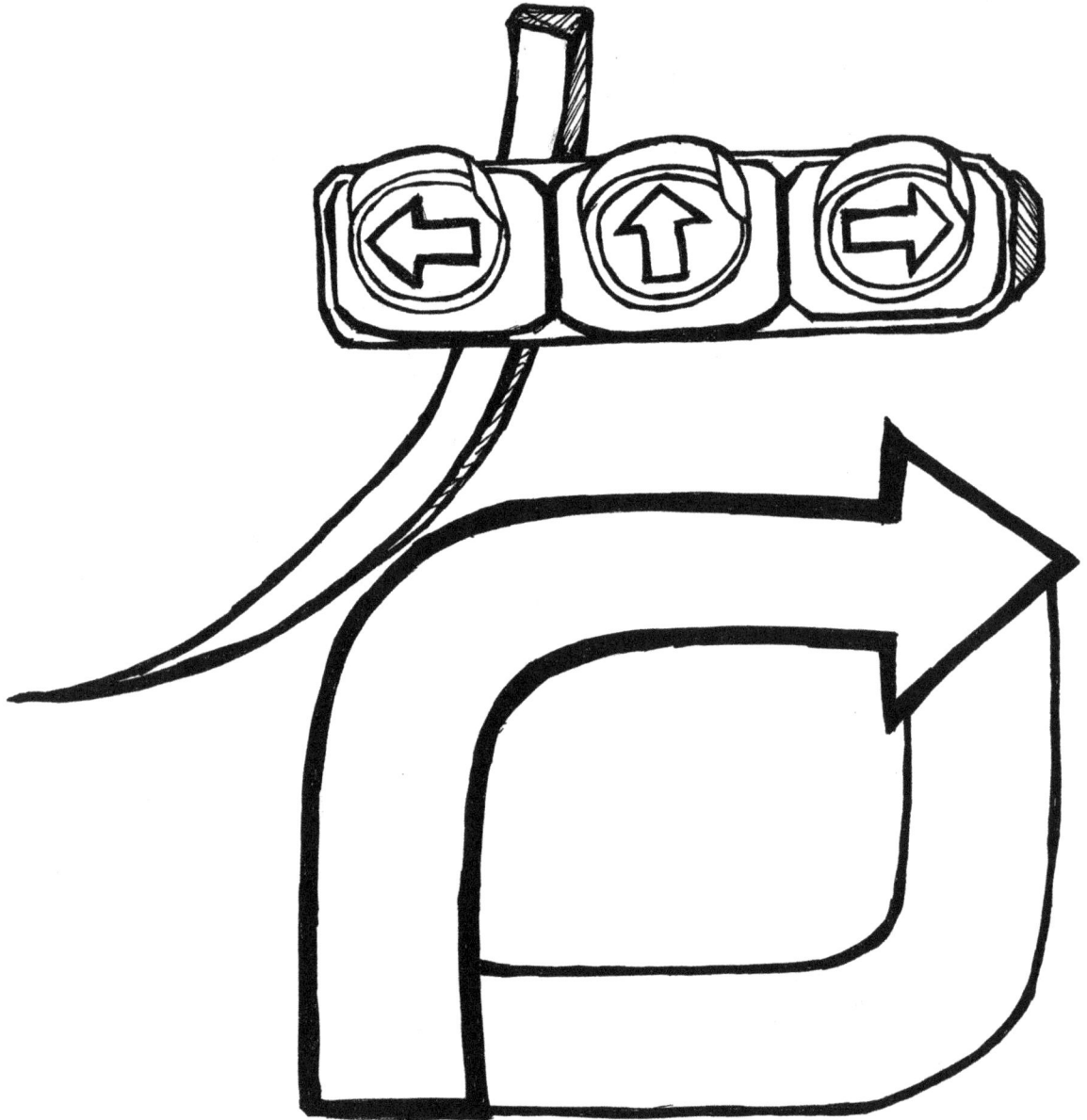

右

yòu

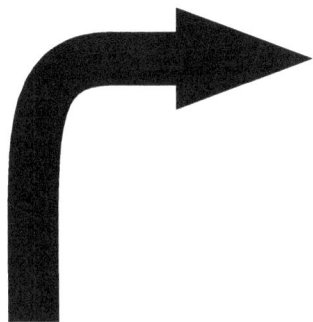

yòu zhuǎn

右转

yòu

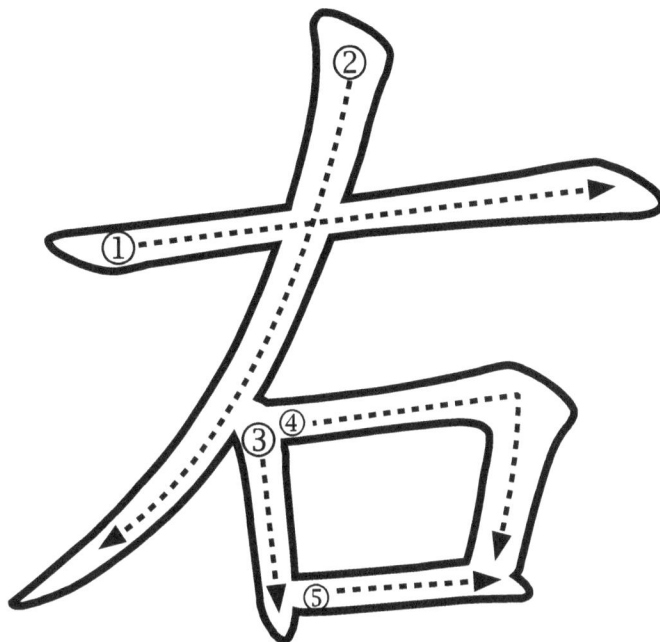

yòu	yòu	yòu	yòu	yòu
一	丆	才	右	右

HAVE

有

yǒu

?

yǒu méi yǒu
有没有

yǒu

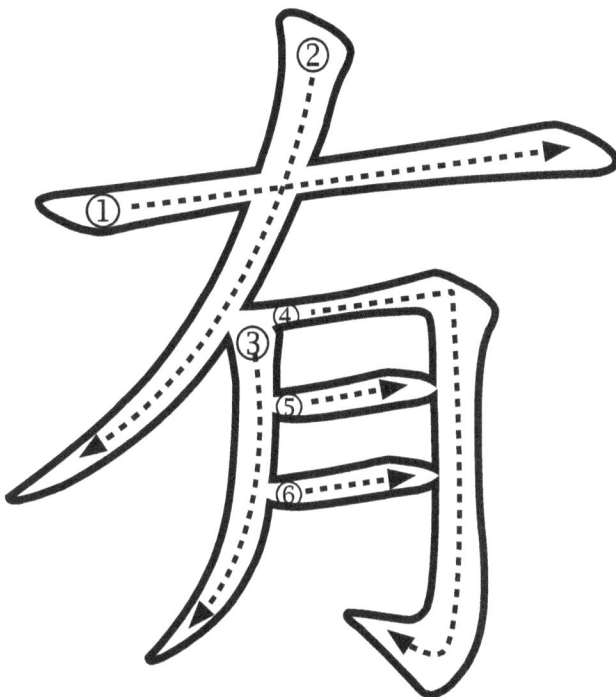

一 ナ 才 有 有

有

SHARP

尖 jiān

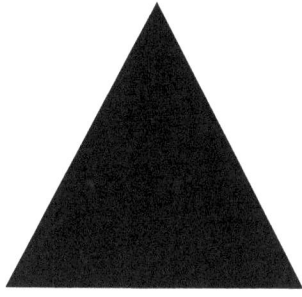

jiān de

尖 的

jiān

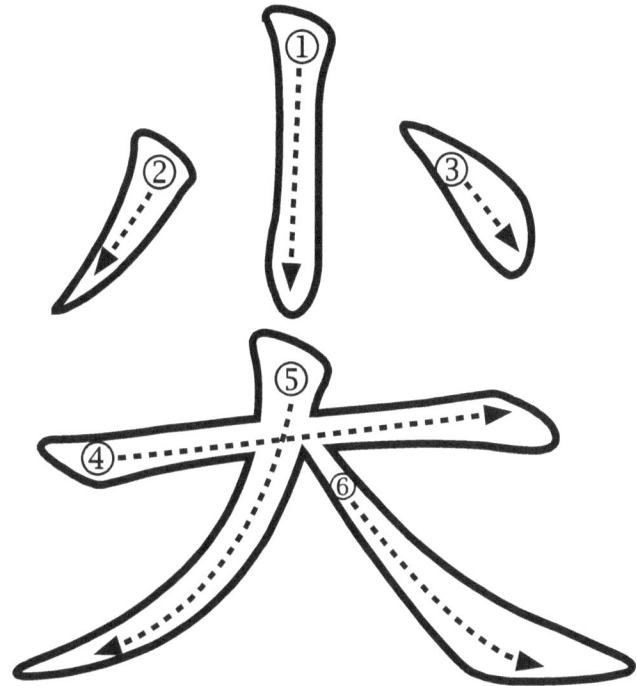

jiān	jiān	jiān	jiān	jiān
jiān				

NO

不

bù

bù   hǎo

不好

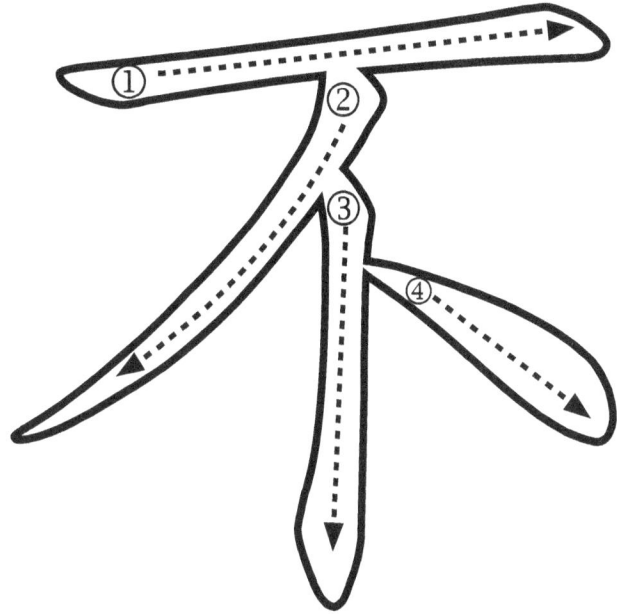

bù	bù	bù	bù	

WOOD

木

mù

shù mù
树 木

mù

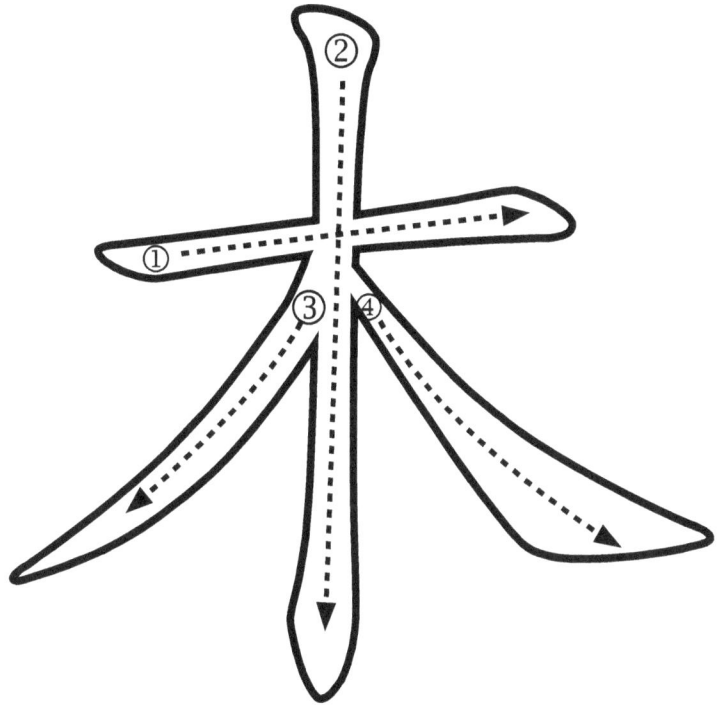

MOUNTAIN

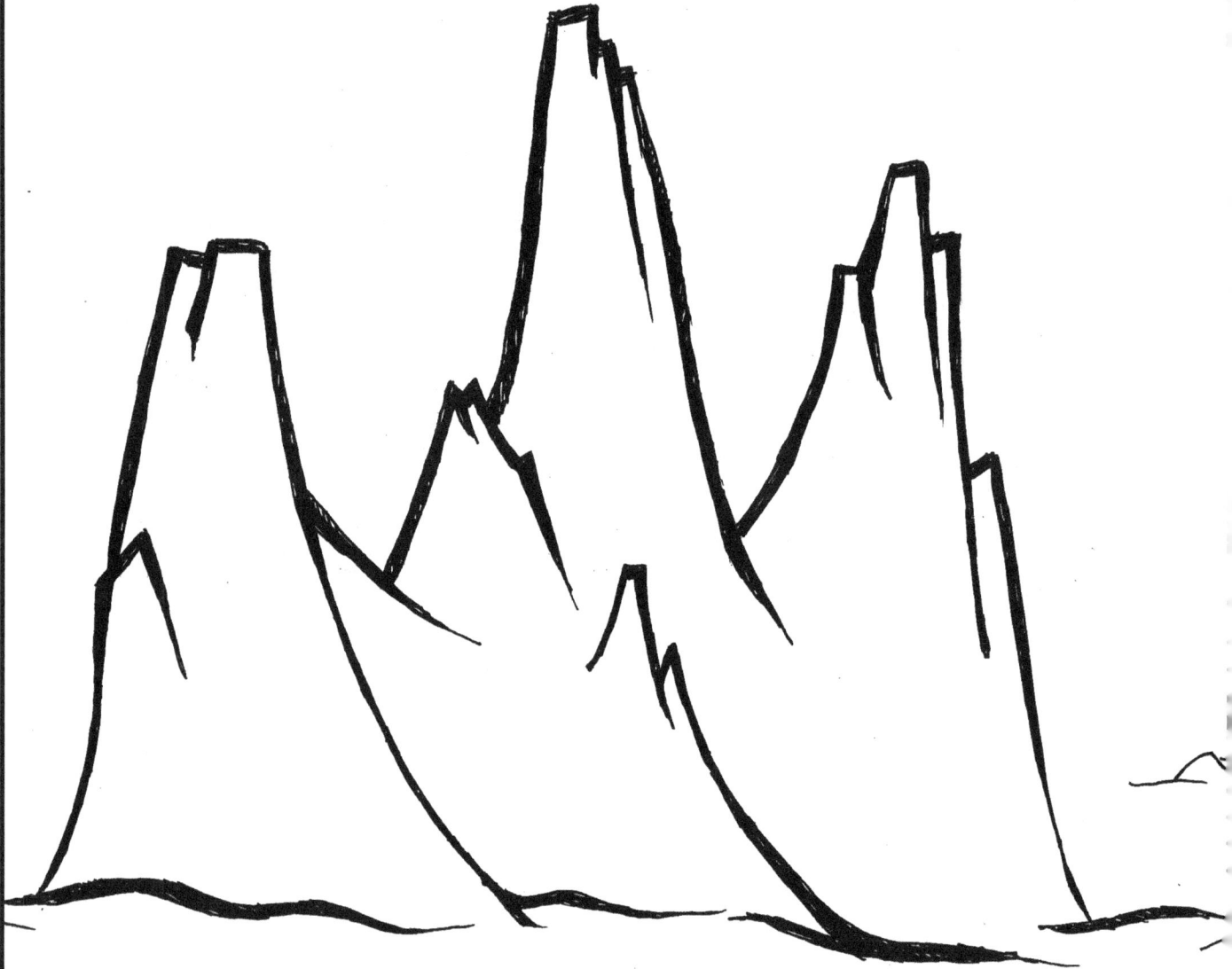

山 shān

gāo　shān

高山

shān

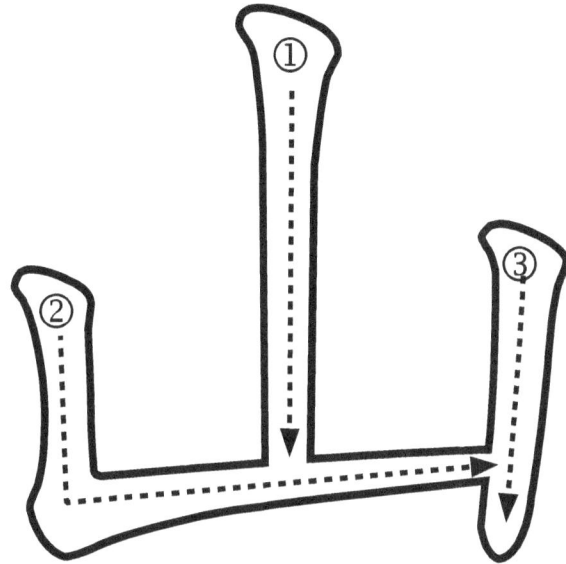

shān	shān	shān		

FIRE

火

huǒ

huǒ

shēng huǒ

生火

huǒ	huǒ	huǒ	huǒ	
丶		少		

WATER

水 shuǐ

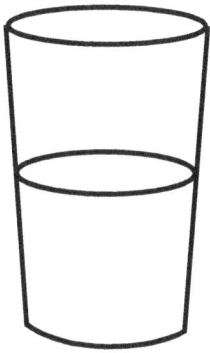

shuǐ

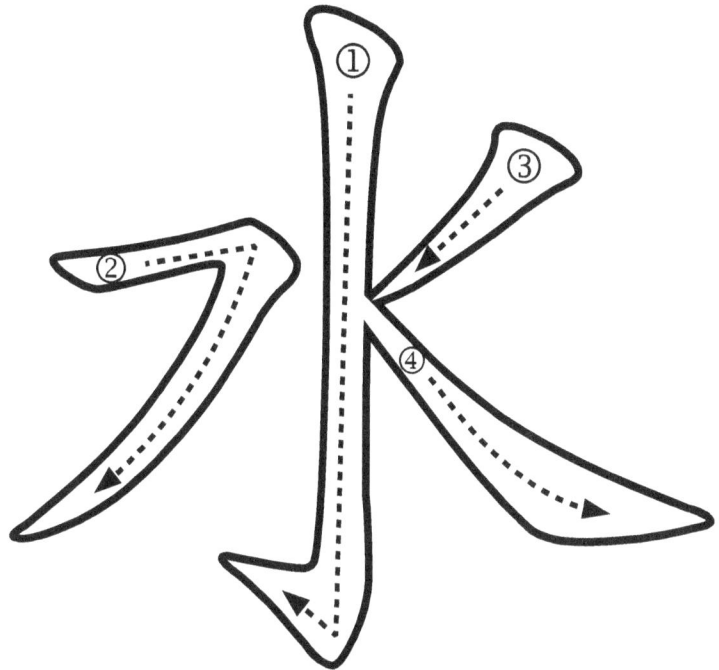

yī　　bēi　　shuǐ

一 杯 水

shuǐ	shuǐ	shuǐ	shuǐ	
			水	

FOREST

林 lín

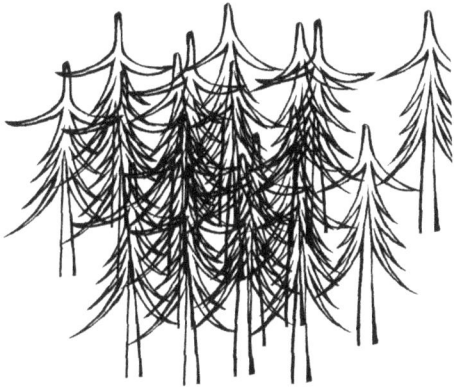

sēn　　lín

森林

lín

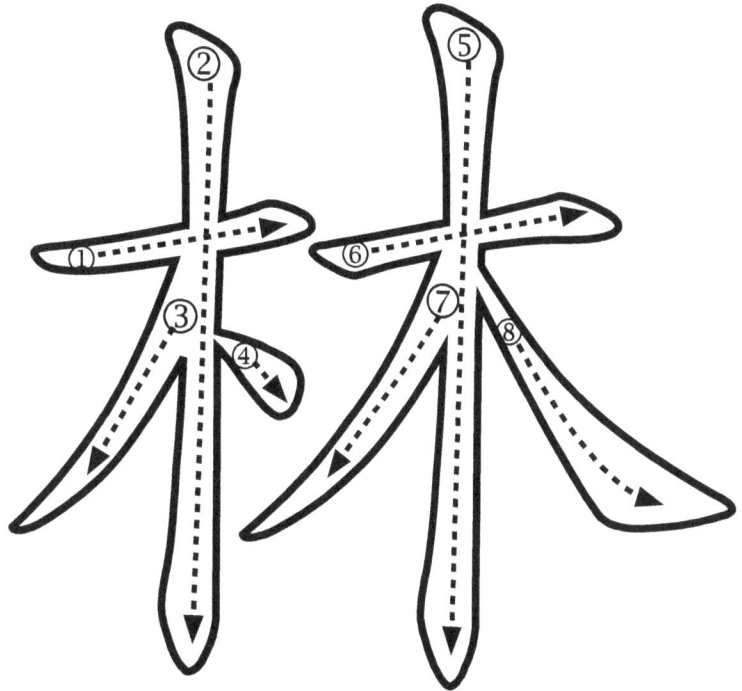

lín	lín	lín	lín	lín
lín	lín	lín		

MOON

月

yuè

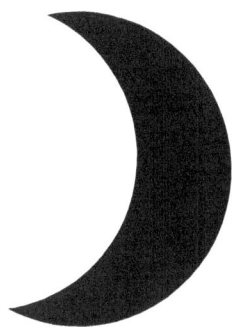

yuè liang
月 亮

yuè

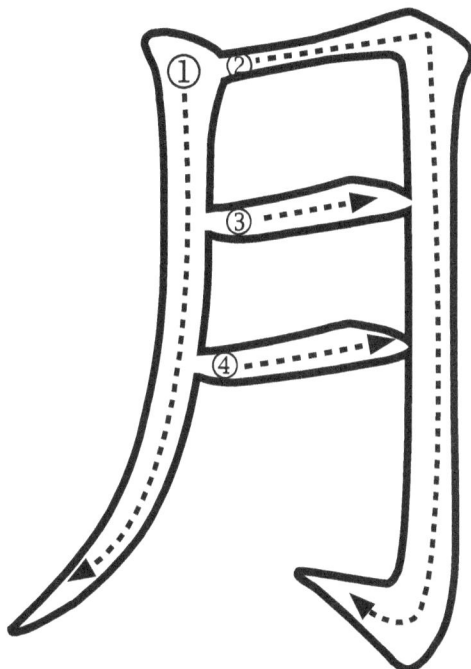

yuè	yuè	yuè	yuè	
			月	

* Pronunciation differences between Traditional and Simplified Chinese. (liàng liang)

EARTH, DUST

土 tǔ

tǔ dì

土地

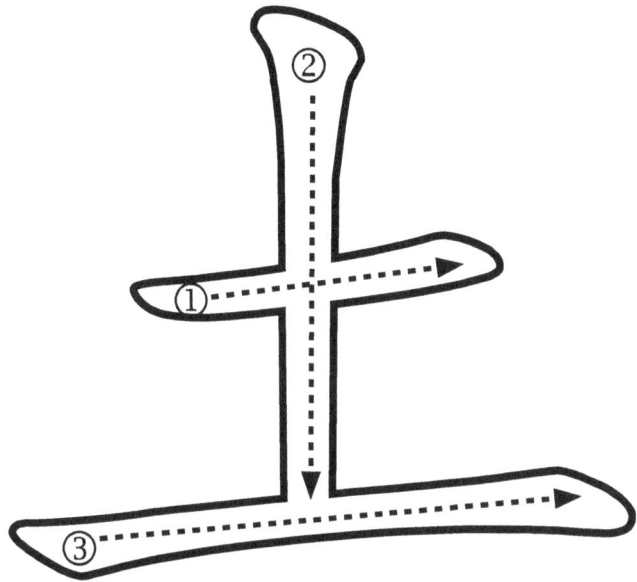

tǔ	tǔ	tǔ		
	十	土		

SKY

天

tiān

tiān kōng

天空

tiān

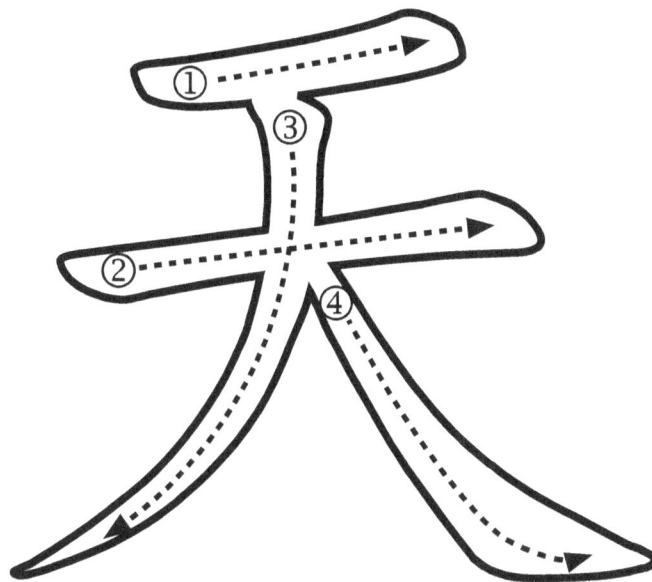

tiān	tiān	tiān	tiān	

BIRTH

生 shēng

shēng   rì

生 日

shēng

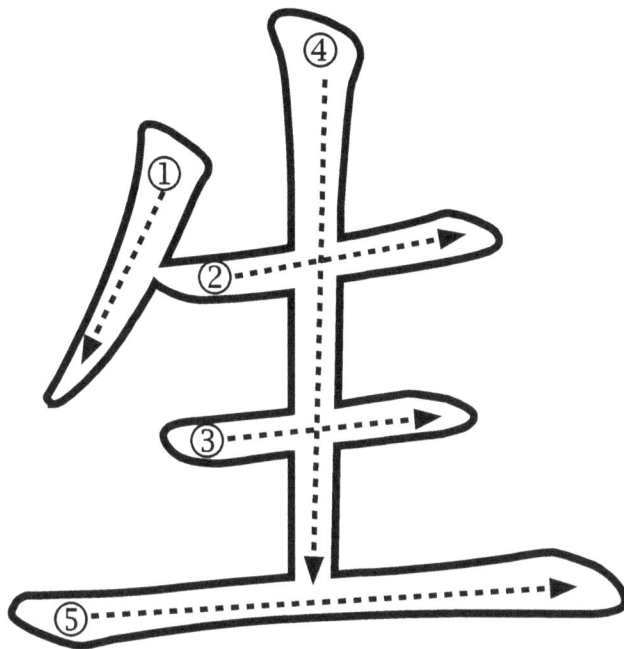

shēng	shēng	shēng	shēng	shēng

SUN, DATE

日 rì

rì guāng

日 光

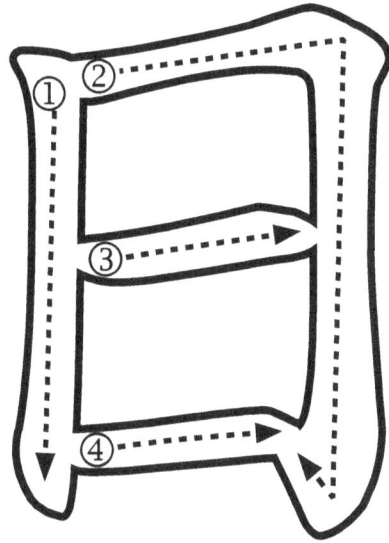

CARD, CHORKED

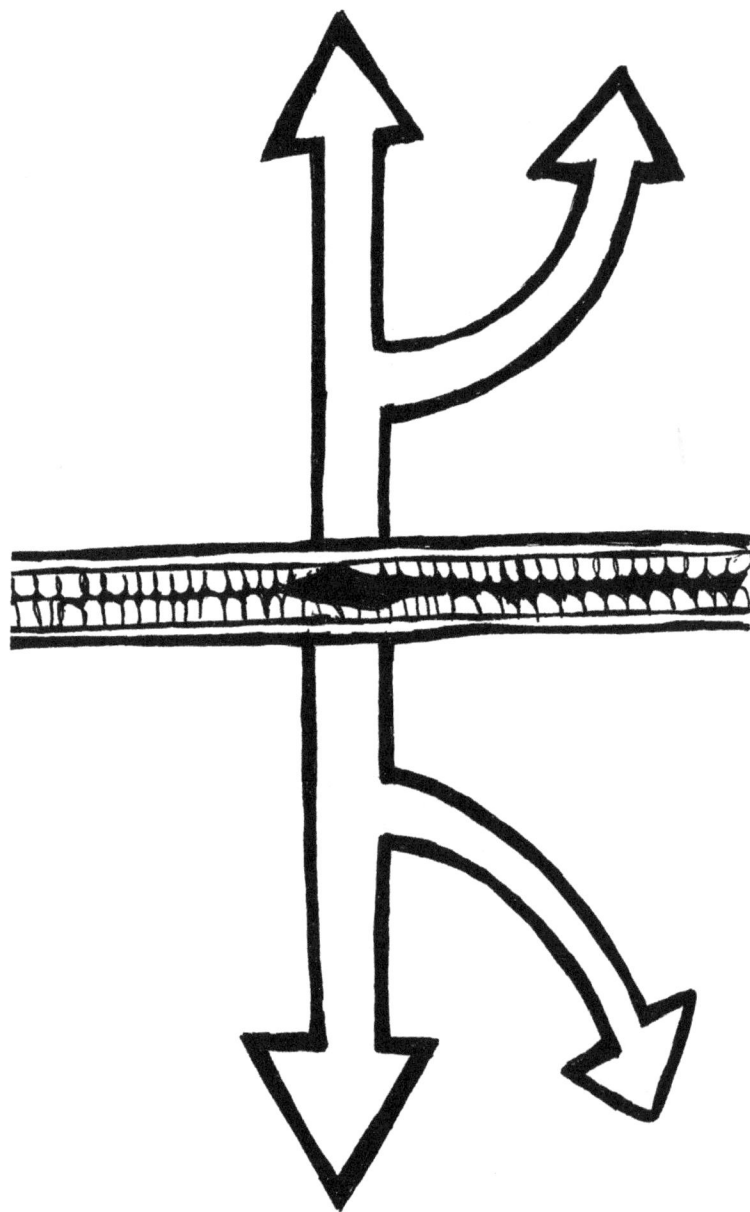

卡

kǎ

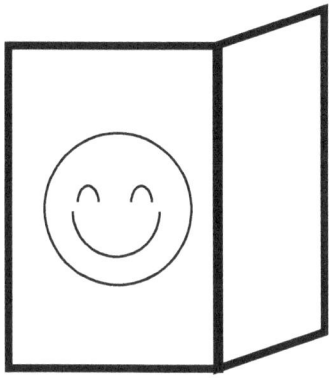

qiǎ piàn

卡 片

kǎ

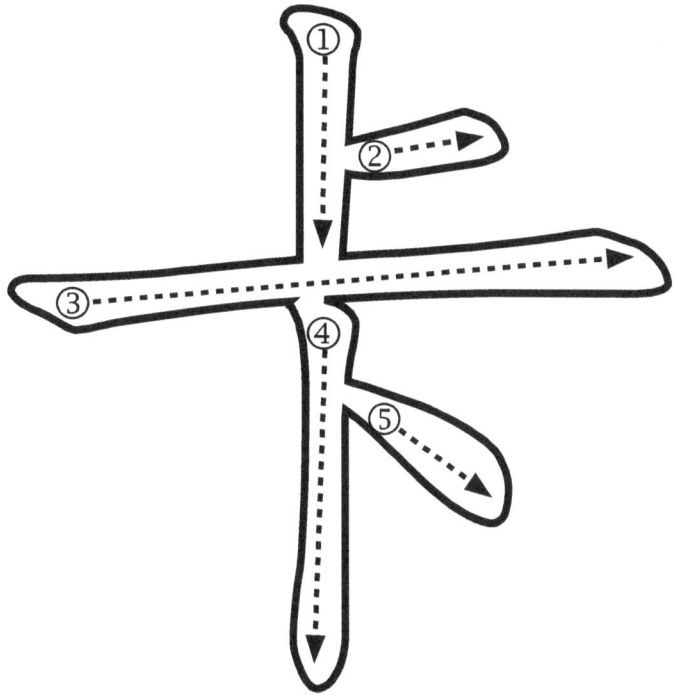

EARLY

早 zǎo

zǎo shàng

早上

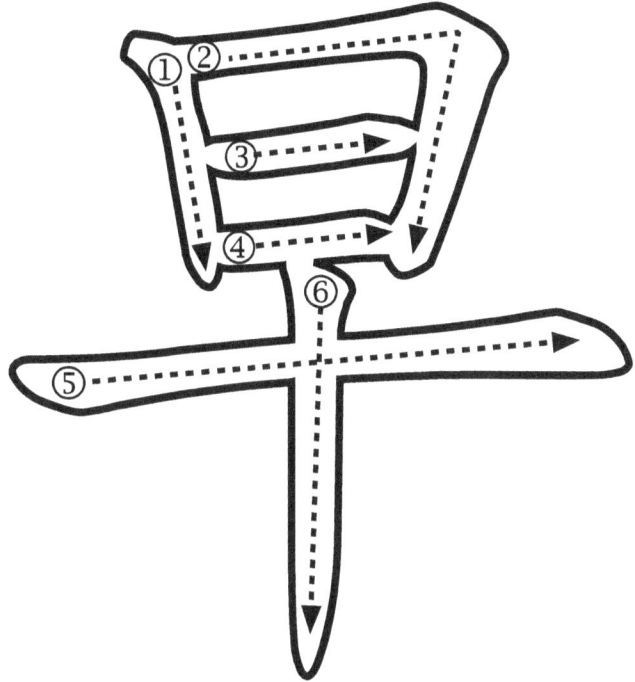

zǎo	zǎo	zǎo	zǎo	zǎo
zǎo				

AISO, TOO

也 yě

yě shì
也 是

yě

yě	yě	yě		

RED

红 hóng

hóng píng guǒ
红苹果

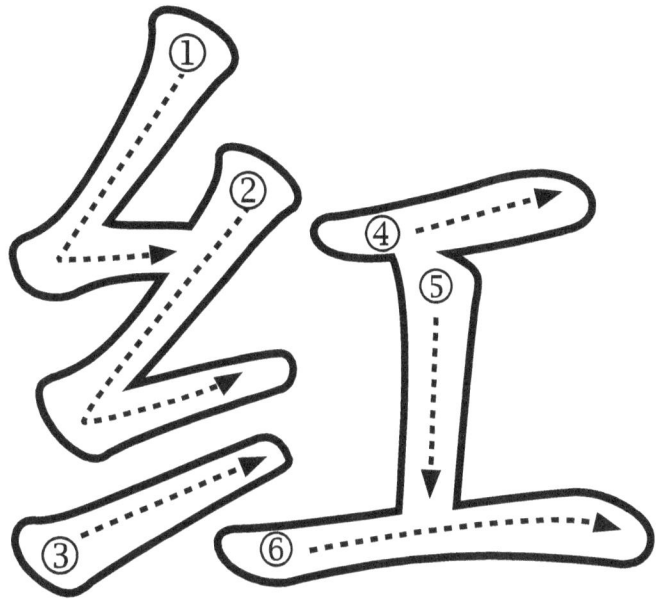

hóng	hóng	hóng	hóng	hóng
纟	纟	纟	纟	纟
hóng				
红				

www.ingramcontent.com/pod-product-compliance
Lightning Source LLC
Chambersburg PA
CBHW081243020426
42331CB00013B/3280